MONTENEGRO

MONTENEGRO

Publisher
INTERSISTEM – Belgrade

Editor
Goran Jovanović

Photography
Dragan Bosnić

Layout
Igor Petrović

Text
Dragan Bosnić

Consulting editor
Dr Stevan Stanković

Translation
Dragana Tošić

Cartography
INTERSISTEM - BELGRADE

Printed
REKLAM Jagodina

ISBN 86-7722-058-5
COBISS.SR-ID 122697740

Montenegro

The story goes that the Montenegrins use four comparison levels for »handsome«. As alleged, they say – ljep, ljepši, najljepši, e viđu mene (handsome, handsomer, the handsomest, but look at me) Weather the "đetići" (»Montenegrin boys«) are so handsome, the ladies who visit Montenegro during the summer (or winter) can check it on but this fourth comparison level could by all means be applied to the region where they live – e viđu te ljepote (look at that beauty). Montenegro covers the most beautiful part of the Mediterranean coast where long, sandy beaches are followed by rocky, hidden small bays with crystal, translucent water. Green conifers, thousand-year-old olives and fragrant Mediterranean vegetation descend to the beaches splashed by wanton waves. Modern hotel complexes fit well with old Mediterranean towns. High mountains tower above the coast, diving directly here and there into the deep blue depths. Running mountain rivers have cut deep, incredibly beautiful canyons through these huge masses. It is rarely snowing at the seaside, and it is rarely thawing on the peaks of the Durmitor Mountain. The usual background of the cheerful march of majorettes clothed in short skirts, are the peaks of the mountains Orijen and Lovćen clad in snow cover. The beauty of Montenegro is omnipresent and visible at every step, from the peak of Lovćen as well as from the highway that follows its tortuous course high in the mountain. A railway track spans the Mala River with a big bridge, climbing up to the highest Montenegrin peaks. Such a diverse landscape within such a restricted area is difficult to find anywhere on the Planet. A significant number of Montenegrin regions are on the UNESCO World Heritage List.

Montenegro

The canyon that the Tara River cuts through the mountain is the second deepest canyon in the world. Nevertheless, while through the Colorado River runs muddy yellow water, the water out of the Tara River is drinkable at any part of the canyon. Though Montenegro covers a rather small area, it has no less than four national parks. In this connection, neither part of an exceedingly beautiful coast is awarded by that label, not even the most beautiful European fjord, Boka Kotorska. There is a plan according to which the Prokletije Massif should become a national park of Albania, Montenegro and Serbia. The Montenegrins are aware of their country's beauty and that's why in 1991 the Montenegrin Government declared it the first ecological state.

Montenegro

Seaside

The most beautiful part of the Adriatic coast that belongs to Montenegro is about 280 km long, not less than 73 km of which is suitable for swimming, and sandy beaches are more than 30 km long all together. These features are subject to change because attractive summer resorts with nicely dressed beaches are arising every day on the most inaccessible parts of the coast. In the coastal area the water temperature is varying from 12°C in February to 25°C in August. More and more tourists are spending their vacations by the neighboring lake of Skadar, where during summer season the water reaches the temperature of 28°C. The Montenegrin seaside stands out with four regions – the region of Boka Kotorska, the region of Budva, the region of Bar and the region of Ulcinj. Each region has its peculiarities, and what they have in common is the warm sea and nice beaches. Boka Kotorska is adorned by old towns and an unusually deep bay bordered with high mountains. Although Perast is some ten kilometers away from the rainiest zone of Europe, it is considered one of the sunniest towns of the Mediterranean. The region of Budva is distinctive by its variety of beaches with nearby town-hotels accompanying them. This is the most vivacious part of the coast, most often visited by young people. The region of Bar has been long time reserved for family and company tourism. Lately, wide beaches and more and more hotels of high quality have become attractive to more choosy guests as well. Ulcinj has its Stari grad (Old town), the longest beach in Montenegro, the nudist island Ada Bojana and a great many small bays that extend from Bar to Ulcinj.

Seaside

Boka Kotorska

The beauty of Montenegro consists of a unique combination of high, wild mountains and the sea that has made many romantic coves and filled them with the finest sand. It seems as if the Creator at one point didn't know how to reconcile those two beauties and that he decided to let them form each other. The sea drew deeply into the land and the high mountains embraced it with a great bear hug. Thus was Boka Kotorska, the deepest and the most beautiful fjord of the Mediterranean created. People have strung there about ten stone towns, white as pearls, and the Adriatic bride was dressed up. The Bay of Boka Kotorska consists of four smaller bays: The Bay of Kotor, The Bay of Risan, The Bay of Tivat and The Bay of Topla. The surface of the Bay is not big (87 km2), but the coast is well indented and over a hundred kilometers long. The narrowest part of the Bay is the Verige strait, about 350 meters wide. In the old days chains ("verige") were stretched here to prevent the enemy's ships from entering the Bay of Kotor and Risan. Today in this area between Lepetani and Kamenari ferryboats run, shortening by thirty kilometers the crossing of the Bay.

Herceg Novi

One of the most beautiful Adriatic promenades Šetalište Pet Danica (The Pet Danica Walk) , seven kilometers long leads us from Meljine to Igalo. At the very beginning of the Walk, in Savinska Dubrava (Savina grove) there is Monastery Savina, dating from the 11th century. Three houses of prayer form part of the monastery complex: The Church of Sveti Sava (Saint Sava Church), the new and the old Church of the Assumption of the Virgin Mary. In the monastery treasury there is a crystal cross, mounted in silver, which, according to legend, belonged to Sveti Sava (Saint Sava). Not far from the monastery, at the location from where there's a view over the whole town, there is a Tomb of the Unknown Soldier. Below the monument, down the slope the walls of Herceg Novi descend all the way to the sea. The town was built by Bosnian king, Tvrtko the First, at the end of the 14th century, and named it Sveti Stefan. In the ensuing years, the town fell under the rule of the Duke of Hum, Stjepan Vukčić Kosača, who fortified it and gave it the name it bears today. The Venetians, Spanish, Turks, French and the Austrians fought over the town and they all added something to the town or tore something down. The seafarers of Herceg Novi sailed all over the world, bringing back exotic plants and building luxurious villas. The famous Kanli kula (Kanli Tower) is today an open-air theatre, and the fort Forte Mare, as well as the Spanish Tower, are covered with palm trees, eucalyptuses, cypresses, agaves, mimosas, magnolias and other exotic plants. From time to time the army of beautiful majorettes marches through the sunny town announcing the Days of Mimosa.

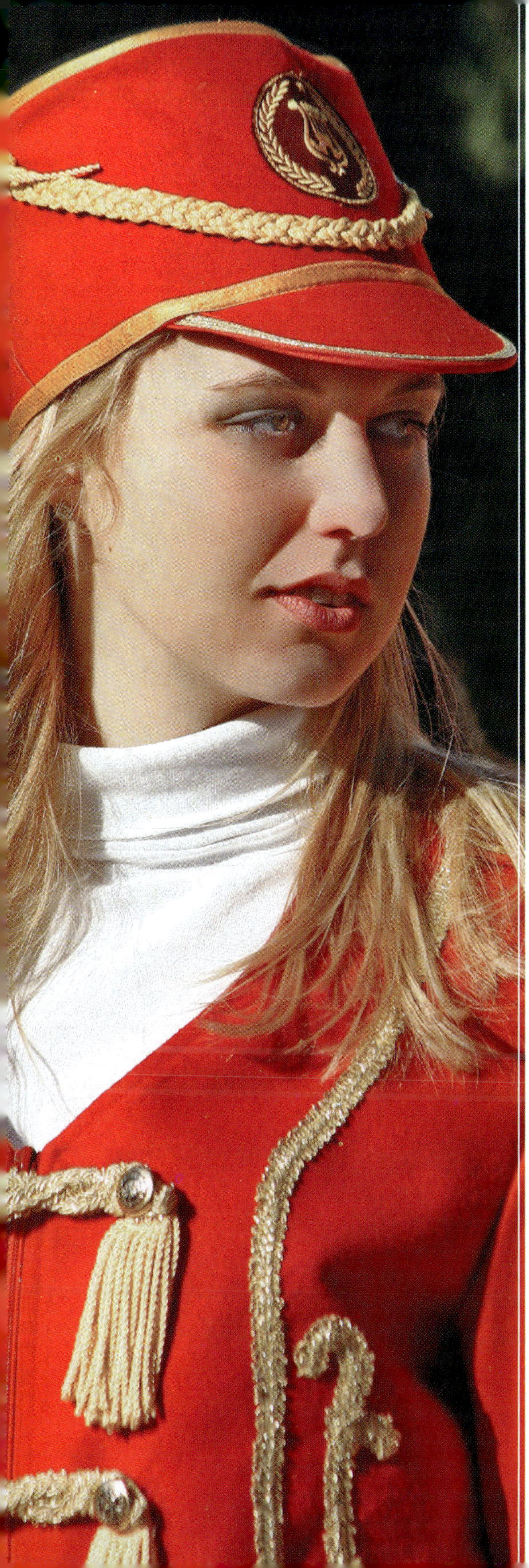

Herceg Novi

The central town square Square of Herceg Stjepan is also called Belavista because of the magnificent view over the Bay. The square is embellished with the Church of Sveti Arhandjeo Mihajlo (Saint Archangel Michael), surrounded by four huge palm trees. On the very beach there are the beach Hotel Plaža, a glass - structure, many coffee-bars and the promenade Pet Danica that leads towards Igalo. This little town has become an important health center for treatment of rheumatic diseases, degenerative alterations of joints and muscles. At the end of the Bay are Njivice and the Prevlaka peninsula. The Island of Mamula guards the entrance of the Bay with a powerful fortress which has never been used for military purposes.

Herceg Novi

Morinj

Morinj, a little settlement has squatted in the greenest part of the Bay. Less than five kilometers away from Perast, but not nearly as sunny as Perast. In the hills overlooking Boka, Crkvice, the rainiest place in Europe is situated; the important part of these precipitations breaks through the Karst ground ending up in the Bay between Risan and Morinj. When the spring Sopot becomes active, the sea level gets considerably increased. A part of that water appears in Morinj. Fresh water that springs directly from the ground was once used to move numerous mills that ground grain and squeezed the juice from olives. Only one mill is still in operation today, the others have been adapted and turned into attractive inns. One of the most popular restaurants in Boka is "Ćatovića mlini". Next to Morinj, in the village Lipci, on a protruded rock, drawings made by prehistoric hunters are still visible.

Risan

Where had precisely those prehistoric hunters – painters from Lipci - lived it is not known, but it is certain that the oldest known historical place is Risan. The fortified Illyrian settlement was mentioned, as far back as in the 3rd century B.C. According to legend, the Illyrian queen Teuta used to hide there from the Roman invasion. The Romans conquered Risan and turned it into a summer residence. A fair number of coins from the Illyrian period, minted in a local blacksmith workshop, are preserved. The Romans left perfectly preserved mosaics, the most beautiful among them being the large mosaic with God Hypnos in a lying position. By the road that leads from Risan to Perast there is Monastery Banja. The monastery church was built by the district prefect of Raška, Stefan Nemanja, who dedicated it to Sveti Djordje (Saint George).

Perast

The town Perast is situated opposite the Verige strait, as an eternal sentry of the Bay of Kotor. The defensive forces of the town were significantly increased by the fortress of Sveti Križ, which is situated on a hillock above the town. Even when the Turks had taken possession of the surroundings of Perast, the town remained spitefully unconquerable. During Napoleon's wars, the French too had most difficulties with the citizens of Perast. From the 14th to the 19th century there was a shipyard, as well as a private naval school. Even the Russian tsar , Peter the Great used to send his cadets to school there. Due to its pronounced baroque architecture, the whole town has been placed under protection of the state.

Perast

In front of the town, like two anchored stone ships, rest two islands: Sveti Djordje and Gospa od Škrpjela. On the Island of Sveti Djordje there is a church of the same name dating from the 12th century, and the graveyard of Perast, and that is probably why it is also called The Island of the Dead. The Island of Gospa od Škrpjela (crags) is an artificial island, and the old tradition of ritual covering of crags with rocks and old barges has been preserved to the present days. The church was built in the 17th century and painted by Tripo Kokolja. In the church there are over two thousand votive church tablets made of silver, left by seafarers who had survived storms or fierce

Perast

Perast

Kotor

The first known settlement at the bottom of the Bay of Kotor was the Greek town of Akurion; the Romans named it Acruvium, and finally, the Slavic tribes gave it the name of Kotor. Since the 9th century the town protector became Saint Tripun. During that period the The Brotherhood of the Seafarers of Boka Kotorska was founded and the citizens from Kotor used to sail in their swift sailboats to all harbors of the world, known at that time. The city kept being on the rise in spite of the Turks, Venetians, Napoleon and a destructive earthquake in 1667. The invention of steamboats, as well as the establishment of a railway connection between Trieste and Rijeka (Fiume) made the Navy of Boka fade away. Just when Kotor and other towns of Boka began to recover, a catastrophic earthquake happened in 1979 and damaged more than 600 buildings of major cultural significance. In the same year UNESCO proclaimed the town of Kotor a universal world heritage monument. In spite of all misfortunes that Kotor was stricken with, the town managed to preserve an atmosphere of a medieval Mediterranean town with narrow, zigzag streets and powerful walls surrounding it. The town is encircled with walls 20 meters high, 2 to 15 meters wide and 4.5 km long. One branch of the wall begins at the harbor, i.e., at the South Gate, the second one at the Škurda river, i.e. at the West Gate, both ending at the fort of Saint Ivan. The Fort towers above the town, with 1426 steep steps leading to it.

Kotor

Near the Fort there is a gate leading to the old Road of Njegos; apart from this gate, the town can be entered into through (are) four other gates. The Main (West) City Gate or the Gate from the sea connects the harbor with the Square of Arms. The gate continues with the Tower of Town Sentry on the right and the Duke's Palace on the left side. Adjoining the Duke's palace there is the Town Inn, built in the place where Napoleon's Theatre once was. Opposite the Main City Gate there is the Clock Tower dating from 1602 and the pyramidal Pillory in front of it. From the Clock Tower to the right towards Cathedral, there are four magnificent buildings ornamented with coats of arms. These are the palaces belonging to the families of Bisanti, Beskuća, Buća and Pima. The Square of the Cathedral is the main town square, where the Historic Archive of Kotor, the City Hall, the Palace of the Drago family, the Bishop's Residence and the (magnificent structure of) Sveti Tripun Cathedral are situated.

Kotor

Since 1166 the Cathedral suffered many changes many times and after the earthquake in 1667 it was renovated and has not been altered ever since. In the Piazza of the salad there is the Palace of Vrakjenovs, the Venetian Military Hospital (Cultural Center) and the Church of Sveti Franja (Saint Francis Church). Behind the church there is the South City Gate which still has counterweights used for lifting the bridge. The North Gate or the Gate of the Rijeka leads across the suspension bridge to the river Škurda. This gate was renovated in the 16th century after the futile Turkish siege of the town. Then the Turkish Admiral Hajrudin Ridjobradi (red beard) turned back his fleet of 200 ships and 30 000 soldiers and, like many before him, left the walls of Kotor empty-handed. By the gate there is the Church of Sveta Marija od Rijeke (Church of saint Mary of the River) from the 13th century.

A bit down below, towards the West Gate there are the Open-air Theatre, the Church of Sveti Nikola (Saint Nicholas Church), the Treasury of the Serbian Ortodox Church and the Church of Sveti Luka (Saint Lucas Church) dating from the 12th century. The Square of Grgurin with The Naval Museum (the palace of Grgurin) is situated between the Saint Nicholas Square and the Square of the Cathedral. The museum is in possession of the richest collection on the East coast of the Adriatic Sea.

Prčanj

Ever since Prčanj was built, its inhabitants were oriented towards the sea. They used to go fishing or to "vijać" – that's how they called their long overseas voyages. The successfulness of their voyages is depicted in luxurious palaces surrounded with exotic plants and in Virgin Mary Cathedral in the city center. The seafarers from Prčanj sailed the seas and their wives waited for them for days, months, years... In Prčanj there is still a three-part house with three windows at which three sisters waited for the same captain. Time was passing by, the first sister died, then the second one too, the captain wasn't coming back. The first window was sealed up, then the second one too. There was no one to seal up the third window. Thanks to the special micro-climatic conditions in Prčanj, a special health institution Vrmac for treatment of bronchitis, asthma and allergic diseases was established.

Prčanj

Tivat

Tivat was mentioned in the ancient times, but as a summer residence of wealthy citizens of Kotor. It obtained the status of the city only after the Arsenal for ship-repairing yard had been started by the Austro-Hungarian Monarchy. At the end of the Bay of Tivat there is Soliolsko polje (Field of Solila) or Solila. It was named after the saltworks from the Middle Ages. Next to the saltworks which are still in operation, there is a civil airport. For tourists arriving by plain the nearest and the most attractive summer resort is Ostrvo cveća (the Island of Flowers). This island with rich vegetation has become a real tourist paradise. Next to the island there is a small island called Gospa with Franciscan convent and a small museum exhibition. The closeness of the airport and tourist complexes along the coast towards Donja Lastva and Krašići make Tivat most attractive holiday destination.

Rose

At the entrance of Boka Kotorska, at the peninsula Lustica, there are some ten beautiful beaches and the attractive Plava špilja (the Blue cave). These beaches can be reached by an asphalt road from Tivat, but faster and more attractive access is by tourist boats from Herceg Novi. At the entrance of the Kumbor straits, in Rose there used to be a quarantine for ships sailing into the bay. That was the place where marry mariners used to leave their concubines, ending their voyages as exemplary husbands. It is lively in Rose today too. In the summer season a lot of rock-concerts are organized in the old navy base. The powerful fortresses of Mamula and Mirište have become an attractive beach decoration and a confident landmark to all vessels entering the Bay of Boka Kotorska.

Rose

Budva

Two thousand and a half years ago the city of Budva had found its place in one of the most beautiful parts of the Adriatic coast. The first settlement was situated on a small island which in time was connected with the mainland. By tradition, it was founded by Kadmo, son of Phoenician King, when he was expelled from Thebae. People say that he reached the Adriatic coast in a bullock cart and established there the city of Budva. The city silhouette is recognizable also by the neighboring Island of Sveti Nikola (Saint Nicholas Island). City walls surround the Church of Sveti Jovan (Saint John Church) from 17th century, Santa Maria in Punta, the Church of Benedictine Monastery from 9th century and the Church of Sveto Trojstvo (the Holy Trinity Church). In front of the last mentioned is a grave of the writer Stjepan Mitrov Ljubiša. Though one of the oldest cities of this part of the Mediterranean, it is a modern town and the capital of Montenegrin tourism. Below new modern hotels, there are old necropolises and the ancient fortress became a piece of stage settings for the famous cultural event Budva – Town Theatre. High level of insolation, large hotel complexes, good entertainment and beautiful beaches make Budva the most popular summer resort of Montenegro. The wide beach of Jaz with a motor camp, the idyllic beach of Mogren and the Slavic beach with the hotel complex of the same name are the sufficient evidence of it. Farther to the south the hotel town Bečići and Rafailovići line a shore, with a long sandy beach.

Budva

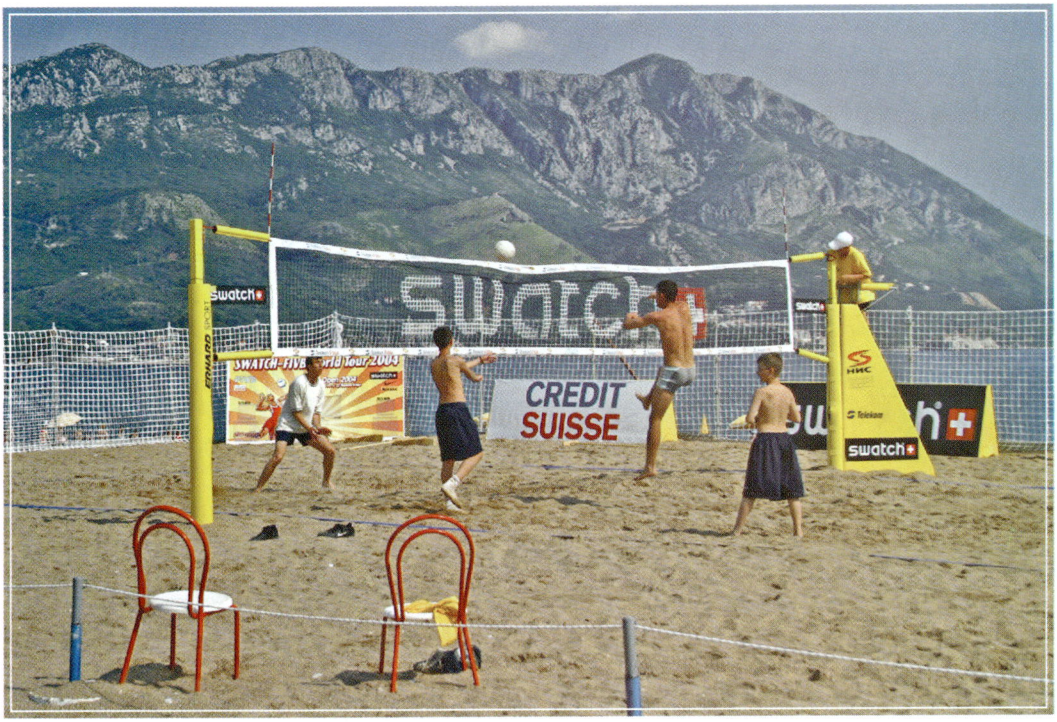

Budva

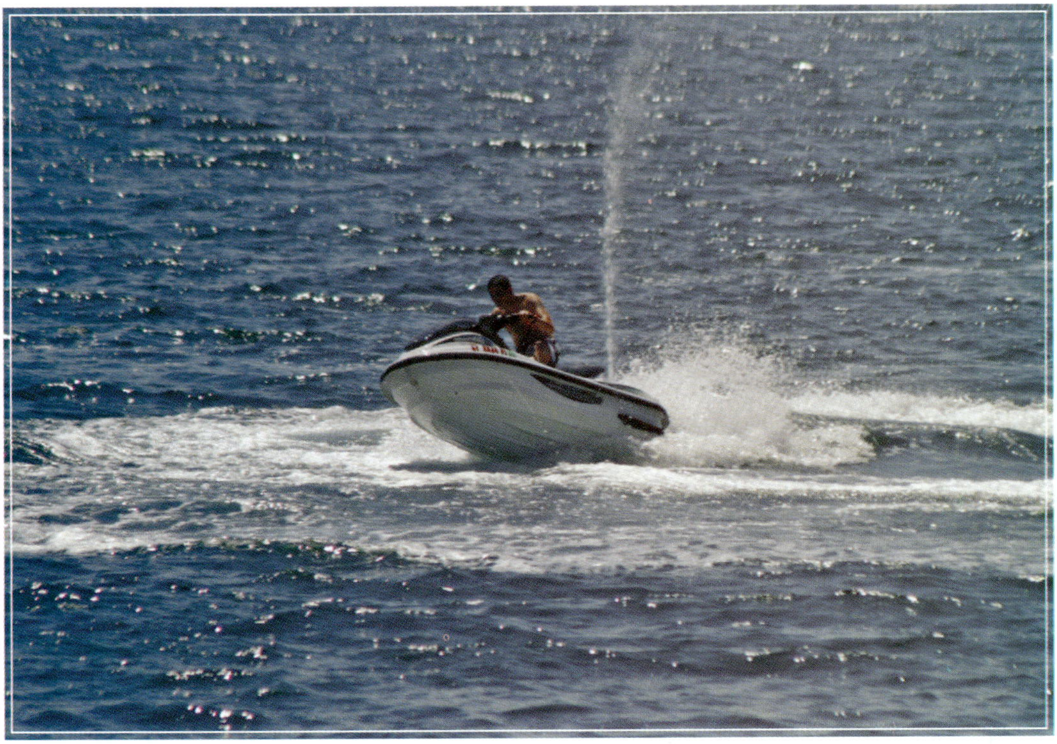

Budva

Budva

Sveti Stefan

To the middle of the past century almost all the inhabitants of the little fishermen island of Paštrovići abandoned it. The painters Milo Milunović and Petar Lubarda saw the picturesque island as a town-hotel intended for wealthy guests. Their idea was supported by tourist-trade workers and in a brief period Sveti Stefan became a summer resort of prestige. There in Sveti Stefan a great number of celebrities found their intimate nook: the English Princess Margaret, former King Umberto the Second of Savoy, writers André Malraux and Alberto Moravia. As it is hard to imagine the jet-set without actors, the island was also visited by Sophia Loren, Doris Day, Sylvester Stallone, Kirk Douglas, Sidney Poitier... One of the most important promoters of Sveti Stefan was the famous model Claudia Schiffer. The isthmus connecting the island with the mainland has become one of the most beautiful beaches of the Mediterranean. Close proximity of the royal summer resort Miločer as well as of the amazing Queen's beach made Sveti Stefan a vision of paradise that many people long for.

Sveti Stefan

Sveti Stefan

Sveti Stefan

Sveti Stefan

Petrovac

Petrovac

Petrovac

Sutomore

Bar

The old urban core of Bar is situated 4 kilometers away from the coastline- The urban core and its suburbs are surrounded with rich vegetation, above all olive groves with trees planted as far back as in the period of Roman rule. People say that young boys from this region couldn't get married before they planted a certain number of olive trees. The city was built far from the sea shore because of a constant pirate threat. Unfortunately, catastrophic earthquakes and explosions of the munitions kept inside the town heavily damaged it, so it was forced to be relocated by the coast.

Later on, the city got a railway connection with Podgorica. By building a large harbor, Bar became the most important communication center of Montenegro. Thanks to good communication lines and beautiful beaches, Bar became an important tourist center.

Bar

Bar

Bar

Ulcinj

The old urban core of Ulcinj is situated in the far south of Montenegrin seaside. It is renowned for its long sandy beaches interrupted with intimate shady beaches, as well as for Old urban core ruled by pirates once upon a time. According to legend, the famous author of "Don Quixote" Cervantes was thrown into terrifying prisons of Ulcinj. Long hot summers, with level of insolation of 11.5 hours a day are alleviated by pleasant sea winds, landward breeze above all. That's why the Big beach of Ulcinj is unimaginable without waves, to the satisfaction of numerous swimmers. Between the Big beach 13 kilometers long and the city there is the Port Milena and the saltworks which cover more than 6,5 million square meters of surface. At the southern side, the Big beach is bordered by the river Bojana and Ada Bojana, the nudist paradise. To the north there is Saško lake, where numerous species of birds have found refuge from the lake of Skadar which has become too noisy; this lake is called *Birds' El Dorado.*

Ulcinj

Ulcinj

Ulcinj

Lovćen

The peak of the mountain Lovćen is contained in the Montenegrin coat of arms. The Montenegrin capital Cetinje is situated below the peak, and at the foot of the mountain there is Boka Kotorska, the most beautiful and the deepest bay of the Adriatic sea. Montenegro has four National parks: Durmitor, a mountain that, like a celestial davit, holds the sky above entire Montenegro; the lake of Biograd, next to the biggest European virgin forest; the lake of Skadar, the biggest habitat of wading birds in Europe, and the mount Lovćen, which leans over Boka like Olympus. Jezerski vrh and Štirovnik are reflected in the dark blue water of the Bay of Boka Kotorska. The deep bay, high level of insolation and high mountains in the hinterland of Lovćen make the clouds, hang in the air above its peak like ice cream scoops. The mean annual precipitation reaches the unbelievable amount of 5.776 mm. As befitting to a huge mountain like this, thunder crashes are habitual, but when clouds part, from Jezerski vrh there's a view all over the Bay of Boka, and when the sky is clear, the Italian coast can be seen as well. At the lower part of Jezerski vrh there is a mausoleum where relics of the greatest mind ever originated from this region, Petar Petrović Njegoš, are kept. The great poet and bishop wanted to be buried at the lower peak because he thought that someone more important than him deserved the upper peak.

Lovćen

Cetinje

Below the peaks of the mountain Lovćen, at the height of 680 meters, Cetinje, the old Montenegrin capital is situated. Cetinje was the last stronghold for Ivan Crnojević, before the invasion of the Turks. He built his palace there in 1482, as well as the Monastery of Cetinje, two years later. Above the monastery there is the Tabalja tower, and in the central city square the fortified palace Biljarda. The most important buildings in Cetinje are Knežev dvor (Duke's Palace) and the street where diplomatic missions of great powers used to be. From the site where the Mausoleum of Njegoš is, there's a view over Cetinje, Boka Kotorska and Njeguši, the village where the bishop was born. In the village there is the Museum of Njegoš, King Nicholas's palace and numerous smokehouses where famous "njeguški prsut" (smoked ham) is smoked.

The Lake of Skadar

As presumed, the lake of Skadar once was a deep bay of the Adriatic Sea; it must have been even more beautiful than Boka Kotorska. Due to the tectonic disturbances, the Rumija mountain went up thus separating the bay from the sea. The only connection left with the sea was the Bojana river, which was slowly deepening its course and lowering the lake level. Because of a big inflow of fresh water by the rivers Morača, Crmnica, Plavnica, Rijeka Crnojevića and of a significant outflow by the Bojana river, the water gradually stopped being salty. Today the lake is filled up with fresh water out of some fifty sources from the bottom, and some of them are below sea level.

The Lake of Skadar

The source Radus is at 90 meters of depth (40 meters below sea level), and that is the deepest point in the lake. The average depth of the lake is five to six meters, but both depth and surface of the lake are changeable - in spring, when snow is thawing, the lake is almost twice as wide and deep as during the rainless period. Thanks to a mild climate, the lake is the biggest winter harbor for birds in Europe. There are often gathered over 270 species, among which is blue heron, black ibises, pochards, pelicans... The lake is proclaimed National park under the UNESCO protection.

The Lake of Skadar

The Lake of Skadar

Rijeka Crnojevića

The Montenegrin people say that Rijeka Crnojevića was made of tears shed by Ivo Crnojević because of the suffering of his people. It is situated in a deep sunken mouth of the river of the same name. It was built on the outskirts of the town of Obod to which Ivan Crnojević moved when the Turks conquered Žabljak.

The first inhabitants were fishermen, and some time later merchants and craftsmen from Podgorica and Skadar came. The King Nikola built his winter residence Ljeskovac there. The old stone bridge, a symbol of the town, dates from that time. The town is famous for its large catch of fish which are canned there too.

Monastery of Ostrog

The Monastery of Ostrog is considered to be one of the greatest consecrated places of the orthodox world. All you need is have a look at lines of barefooted worshippers climbing the rocky ground of Bjelopavlić from the plain valley of the Zeta river to the monastery that like an aerie found a comfortable place on a cliff several hundred meters high. The believers are supposed to sit up the whole night at the plateau in front of the church before they are ready to march-past the reliquary with remains of the great saint, Vasilije Ostroški. One might believe or not in miraculous healings, but the fact is that, apart from those who believe, unbelievers can also be seen here. It is obvious that this peculiar place, high above the peaceful valley, leaves a profound impression and everyone can find his moment of peace there.

Mrtvica

Through the high rocky mountains of Montenegro the abundant water penetrates deeply to the foot of the hill. In time, strong sources have dug deep inaccessible canyons. Except for the wide and plain valley of the Zeta river, the adjoining Bojana river and (at) the Lower Morača, other river valleys are almost impenetrable. The Cijevna river has cut through the plain Cemovsko field a narrow, deep canyon. The canyons of Piva and Komarnica are inundated; through the canyons of Morača and Lim the communication lines are cut through, and the canyon of the Tara river, due to its extraordinary beauty, has been proclaimed National park. The Mrtvica river has cut through the Maganik massif a deep canyon which sporadically is 1600 meters deep, which means that it's even deeper than the Tara canyon. During summer period the Mrtvica river runs dry in its upper flow, but in early spring it is richer in water than the Morača river, which it flows into. People say that once during a spring impact the river overflowed the village Velje Duboko, when it got its gloomy name*.
(*"mrtav"= dead)

Mrtvica

Bjelasica

The National park Biogradska gora was founded by King Nikola in 1878, only six years after the proclamation of the first National park in the world (the Yellowstone in USA). The National park of Biogradska gora is the most afforested park in Europe, with trees more than 400 years old. It is one of three remaining European virgin forests. A part of the National park is also the shady lake of Biograd, surrounded by centuries-old beeches and a pathway. The mountain lakes – forest eyes – complete the beauty of the mountain.

Bjelasica

Bjelasica

Komovi

Komovi is neither the highest nor the most beautiful massif of Montenegro. Yet, the unreal sight of two mountain peaks watched from the distance could be compared only with the view from those peaks of the distant open spaces. The height of 1800 meters, the saddle of Štavna , is reachable only by asphalt road. From that point two peaks – Kučki and Vasojevića Kom tower above up to nearly 2500 meters. What makes these peaks exceptional and incredibly beautiful can be noticed only by mountaineers to whom Komovi is a favourite destination. From the saddle of Carina, at the height of 2300 meters, there are no more signs of any vegetation, and the sight looks like a Moon surface, provided the Moon surface is so brutal at all. At clear weather there is an excellent view from Komovi of the Prokletije massif and of the innumerous peaks of other Montenegrin mountains.

Prokletije

Beautiful but damned*. That's the first thing the inhabitants of these mountains will tell you. No wonder when it is well known that this is the most extended and the highest massif of the whole former Yugoslavia. That's probably why it is called *Balkan Alps*. Mountain peaks over 2500 meters high and mountain lakes surrounded by dense forests, vulnerable only to thunders and the course of time, are what makes the Prokletije massif beautiful. The vicinity of the sea and the high mountains cause capricious climate conditions, what, along with bad roads and the presence of the border that cuts mountain heights, makes the mountain difficult to get to. At the foot of the Prokletije there is an old town Plav, famous for its long history and a beautiful lake on the shore of which it is situated. Out of the lake, the Lim river runs out, and the lake is a real paradise for fishermen. People say that a huchen that weighed 41 kg was caught angling once.

*("proklet"=damned)

Prokletije

Durmitor

Half a century ago almost 40.000 hectares of the most beautiful part of Durmitor and the Tara canyon was proclaimed the National park, protected by UNESCO. Much earlier, King Nikola Petrović proclaimed the area around the Black lake a King's forest preserve. King Nikola was the first official mountaineer of Durmitor, only that he overcame the steep climb to Savin kuk on horse. A great hero Duke Momčilo used to ride his flying horse Jabučilo over the Durmitor. His unfaithful wife Vukosava seemed to be the only person not charmed by the Durmitor. During the creation of Durmitor, the Creator was more than generous. But he hid that beauty over high peaks, deep valleys, narrow canyons, icy caves and remote lakes. He placed magnificent Black lakes on an accessible terrace near Žabljak. Later on he carved out the Savin kuk and the Medjed over them. From these almost inaccessible peaks, the lakes seem infinitely more beautiful. To reach the Sava peak there is a cable-way which makes it possible for the less persistent to enjoy the view of forest eyes surrounded by infinite coniferous woods . From the Savin kuk there is a completely new view of Durmitor massif. Among lots of rocks and peaks stands out the Bobotov kuk, the highest peak of the Durmitor. It is a desired destination for many visitors of this mountain.

Durmitor

Durmitor

Tara

He, who has never tried to raft on white waters of Tara, hasn't sensed a real touch of nature. The overgrown canyon cliffs and lots of springs complete the picture of the untouched nature. Once upon a time people used to raft on real rafts made of wooden logs, what was more challenging but wetter as well. Today big life-rafts for ten persons are used, and rafting is organized on the section starting from Splavište to Šćepan polje. In two days one can cover a distance of almost hundred kilometers. The only intruder over the river is the bridge on Djurdjevića Tara, but it is such effectively built in the landscape, that it doesn't seem as a strange body. When the bridge was built, in 1940, with 366 meters of range and 156 meters of height above the river, it was the biggest road-bridge in Europe.

Tara

Maglić

The north-west part of Montenegro, over Župa Pivska, with the mountains Volujak, Maglić, Vučevo and Bioč, belongs to the National park Sutjeska. The major parts of the Park are located in Republika Srpska, but the most attractive ones are in Montenegro. A rock four hundred meters high, called Kuk by natives, and the river source of Sutjeska at its bottom, are within the territory of Montenegro. The river then crosses the border and through a steep and deep canyon flows into the Drina river. The virgin-forest Perućica is also a part of the Park, with centuries-old trees, whose peace and silence are interrupted only by the high waterfall Skakavac. The few visitors are mostly fascinated by the heart-shaped lake of Trnovac. Many people think that the lake under the foggy peak of Maglić is the most beautiful Montenegrin lake, but at the same time the most difficult to get to.

Maglić

Contents

Montenegro	4
Seaside	10
Boka Kotorska	14
Herceg Novi	16
Morinj	22
Risan	24
Perast	26
Kotor	32
Prčanj	38
Tivat	42
Rose	46
Budva	50
Sveti Stefan	58
Petrovac	66
Čanj	72
Sutomore	74
Bar	76
Ulcinj	80
Lovćen	86
Cetinje	90
The Lake of Skadar	92
Rijeka Crnojevića	98
Monastery of Ostrog	100

Contents

Mrtvica 102

Bjelasica 106

Komovi 110

Prokletije 112

Durmitor 114

Tara 118

Maglić 122